Sold Bunnion

CW01666588

JAMAIC

Books by Andrew Salkey

NOVELS

A Quality of Violence
Escape to an Autumn Pavement
The Late Emancipation of Jerry Stover
The Adventures of Catullus Kelly
Come Home, Malcolm Heartland

SHORT STORIES

Anancy's Score

NON-FICTION

Havana Journal
Georgetown Journal

ANTHOLOGIES

West Indian Stories
Stories from the Caribbean
Caribbean Prose
Young Commonwealth Poets '65
(*Caribbean Section*)
Breaklight
Caribbean Essays

CHILDREN'S NOVELS

Hurricane
Earthquake
Drought
Riot
Jonah Simpson

A READER

The Shark Hunters

Andrew Salkey

JAMAICA

HUTCHINSON OF LONDON

HUTCHINSON & CO (*Publishers*) LTD
3 Fitzroy Square, London W1

London Melbourne Sydney Auckland
Wellington Johannesburg Cape Town
and agencies throughout the world

First published 1973

This book has been set in Times New Roman type, printed in Great Britain on Antique Wove paper by Benham & Co. Ltd., Colchester, and bound by Wm. Brendon & Son Ltd., Tiptree, Essex

ISBN 0 09 115741 2

To
Pat, Eliot and Jason

CONTENTS

I into history, now

You see all them
sweet, young fuck walkin'
'cross over so,
over by the drygoods store?

You did know say
that none o' them
know how much history
under them skin,
coil up inside, there so,
like baby hold back from born?

You did know say
that none o' them
or you
know how much them
an' you
an' me
go through,
how, when, how long,
what for
an' where we goin'?

You see all them
rass gal jus' givin'
all o' we cock-stan',
an' movin' easy,
sof', cool breeze,
an' droppin' shadow
where them don't belong?

Is that, yes!

You did know say
that none o' them
get teach good,
how the history go,
goin' an' gone?
An' goin' come back
an' fuck we, one time, *bap?*

We don't got not'ing
that we can call we own!
We don't 'ave a t'ing!
We's empty people,
wit' not a single 'chievement
f'dog bark wit'!

An' guess who teach them
an' you
an' me
all that slackness?

Nuh more tormented, twis'-up,
brain-wash Black teacher them
than foreigner,
'cause the System stay same way,
like gully-mout',
dark as *rass.*

Is so, yes!

An' what you think goin' 'appen
to all them sweet piece o' pussy
you see walkin'
over so?
An' them gal an' bwoy pickney them?

Them same one know
but them not tellin' a Malcolm soul!

Is only time, rockstone, cutlass,
gun an' some class o' bomb in we arse
goin' catch the gal an' bwoy them,
you an' me,
in a sweet *rass* change o' clothes,
an' wit'out Sunday come, too.

I sittin' down,
scratchin' me 'ead
an' watchin' the scene,
an' I ol' as Anancy
but wit'out f'him brain-box,
an' I say to meself,
"Is how the *mento* music go?"

All o' we losin' out,
'cause we won't own up to weself,
grab we soul,
grab weself like we know weself,
an' tradition-up we tradition,
an' fuck the nex' man
who laugh after we
an' say it small
an' slave-make
an' fragment-up
an' dark night as Dung'll
an' client-tie
an' don't got no industry
an' no technology.

Fuck him, yes!

Culture come when you buck up
on you'self.
It start when you' body make shadow
on the lan'
an' you know say
that you standin' up into mirror
underneat' you.

I say to meself,
"Is how the *mento* music go?"

You say,
"Is how the river flow?"
or, "How the sea does lay down so?"

Don't bother wit' all like me,
Mister Ignorance!

I done wit' you.
I into history, now.
Is not'ing but song I singin'
an' name I callin'
an' blood I boilin'
an' self I raisin',
in a correc' Anancy form,
a t'ing I borrow
an' makin' me own,
wit'out pretty please
or pardon.

Yes, Papa D.,
is me this!

All o' you jus' better start f'make
all the t'ings you use,
'cause the music sayin', "Know you'self!"

So, look inside
an' haul out you'self
an' make a way in the worl',
'cross all the shadows them.
Is only you one you got.
You don't want no help.
You got it
plait up
an' hidin' deep inside you' 'ead.

Is malachite in the sea!

Yes, Papa D.,
is me this;
is me;
is me an' the sea!

1

Caribbea

Xaymaca

. . . thrashing with brute pain
this sea I breathe.

Derek Walcott From 'Tarpon' in THE CASTAWAY

Xaymaca

(i)

Caribbea,
knowledgeable,
patient,

raise your emancipated arms;
give your breasts,

maternal,
absolute,
elegant,
malachite eyes.

Caribbea,
moving in the morning,
shift your pearls;
bolster Xaymaca.

Our Sea,
prepare a path.

When the Doctor Breeze
and the Undertaker Wind
guess your age,
I see you wince;
I feel the shame you bear;
I, too, shudder,
knowing your age,
banded as the coconut palm.

I remember you aging like the coffee bean,
when the Arawaks screamed your name;
when, through the swift, slanting *arbaletes*
stinging the palpitating ground,
Port Maria bared her cocoa brown teeth
and Columbus found a wall of ghosts;

when, after scratches from lobster-claw,
curry-combing from hurricanes,
scorching lashes from city-blaze,
your mangrove arms waved with scars
left by tender, tearing snails;
when lolling *hamacs* swung to stranger winds.

Caribbea,
elegant, in spite of the persistent drill,
galleon-rakings,
ill-timed guffaws from Spanish saints,
your broad face, lashed with thin spume
like Castilian tiaras,
remained still,
full with malachite eyes, searching,
for ever searching,
patient,
couchant.

(ii)

Xaymaca,
troubled child
at Caribbea's side,
soon, the reflection of your image,
your nakedness
was to swing an aimless echo
around an empty room;

yet, then you walked in dream-silk,
spun in suffering,
while the corn-rose stood white
and drained.

Xaymaca,
there was a naked truth
about native feet being made from native clay,
when *Tainos* trowelled at cassava roots
and *Caciques* moved in a Carib calm.

Cashew tree not bearin' guava!

I know that,
under the embroidered skirts, silver buckles,
those marching feet,
you looked up
and gave what you had.

Marked up,
even from then,
death,
number three in our dream,
moved to the tune
of cane shoots,
sending yellow webs
across your face.

Our history,
yours and mine,
a spliced passage,
was music;
and there were mounting murmurs, too,
music on family drums,
drums that gonged, that belonged,
that described Xaymaca's paradox:
come, trample me; come, destroy,
so I might suck the sapling pith,
so I might build from broken stones.

Caribbea,
you knew Xaymaca's ignorance
of one master's smile, another's knife;
you watched her throw her fruits
to the waiting, open mouths,
with the innocence of a smiling child.

Dry 'tump o' cane-piece no f'laugh
when green cane-piece catch fire!

The names,
Oristan and Melilla,
written on and off with blood,
battles that bridged regret
to cracked ways of freedom,
sprang from Don Pedro d'Esquimel's orders
black as Braganza beards,
while the Filibusters served their Corsair sauce;

Hatos: Morante, Ayala, Guanaboa,

opened to harrow teeth,
were gnawed
at rat-pace
behind Melgarejo's back.

To you,
these names are dust and sand,
old sand from sinking columns,
swirling out
of sculptured arches;
they've left their sounds
fixed along a line at night,
explaining the massacre-hush
bouncing off the bare walls
of Sevilla d'Oro's
so-called "pristine splendour",
and remaining behind
guards hovering
over a black quadrille;

and for you
who saw it all,
the sun has become a brilliant
Willy penny,
and the cartridge-worm continues
to forage,
hard as the heart of Harär.

(iii)

There was that spark
that moved the land,
that rumbling, shifting,
accustomed response,
while you,
knowledgeable,
patient,
watched the pelican
rip breast to belly;

Xaymaca,
provident,
paradoxical,
poor child of a thousand loves;

Caribbea,
leaping levator,
muscle to prise up
the granite structure
out of our weakest dreams,
elegant,
maternal,
instead of making us burn
in the drylands of failure,
day after day,
instead of that alternative,
lose the peak
deep inside you;

Caribbea,
victim of careless systems,
absorber of blows,
hear the cry
from Diablo's bedrock,
from the brutally shaved heads
crowding our festering tenements
soon to be planned for,
soon to be bulldozed;

Caribbea,
prepare a path.

Soon your scorpion-times
would be sucked in
by somebody's passing interest
or other,
then, spat out, again,
a step nearer another banner's stab,
the breaking of newer marl stones;

soon names like Penn and Venables
would, with the new course of Conquest,
run rivers, everywhere,
through your shell-marked yards;

soon a swarm of hands
would pass over already teased spots,
pressing a passion
that had flared in panic,
reluctantly,
and died of apathy;

soon the Treaty of Madrid,
merely a moment
in a nasty past
(sordid tests
of hit-and-miss colonization),
would sink its prongs
into a bloody feast;

soon names like Xaymaca
and San Jago de la Vega
would be eased out,
silenced,
shelved:
". . . *well-wooded and watered.*"

Caribbea,
knowledgeable,
patient,

raise your emancipated arms;
give your breasts,

maternal,
absolute,
elegant,
malachite eyes.

Caribbea,
know we ask.

Maternal Sea,
prepare that path.

If we ignore
tek care, the Mother o' safety;
if we ignore
tek time, knock sof'ly;
if we ignore
the real bad ol' daytime dreams them;
if we ignore
han'cuff han' an' han'cuff brain,
and blow *abeng* and fight long enough
in the tall grass,
and go back home to the Cockpit Country
and blow *abeng*, again, and fight long enough
in the pleats and twists of the hills,
would we become
the first Jamaicans,
really become them,
and move on?

Our Sea,
prepare that path.

If we're to play
a game of retroactive yo-yo
with one historical name
or another;
if we're to recall
one bitter price
and put out of our minds another;
if we're to indulge
a bounce back marble circle,
would we be able to fracture
history's pain,
in a drop-pan throw,
salvage all,
and win back ourselves
for ourselves?

Time says no;
we must move on.

Our Sea,
prepare that path.

2

Slavery To Liberation

Because of 1692 Because of 1796
Because of 1833 Because of 1865
Because of 1907

Sooner or later.
But mus'.
The dam going to bus' and every man will break out
and who will stop them?
The force?
What force can stop this river of man
who already know their course?

Bongo Jerry From 'Sooner or later' in *Savacou* 3/4,
Special Issue, December 1970–March 1971

Because of 1692

Port Royal,
flawed peninsula,
very nearly
an offshore island,

chained
but bucking
like land's-end madness,
strip of raw history,
you were violently proud
of the wrecked young
round your neck,
bitten-into lips,
chewed fingernails,
pregnant women with fuller (qualms),
waiting
all waiting
for an uncertain delivery;

your imbricated skin,
slack limbs
certainly couldn't hide
the cancer of the Coast,
the imperial *imprimatur*,
materialism, sanctioned and nailed:
see Gawd dey! me a-tell you
the lan' don't belong to we, at all!

You've been a *palizada*
of all sorts:
"*. . . of wealth, guile, lust*",
of those pretty pennons
rammed into puffed bellie
a thin front line
for Kingston Harbour's
mercantile play.

Port Royal,
you've always been rigid
with presentiment,
sprawling,
expecting the gull's:
"*. . . blood, doubloons and lace.*"

Port Royal,
grounded mockery of a sailing city,
you wore your lashes well;
you screamed
when they were all gone,
but,
after they'd left,
you began to sink:
jus' when you was a-ketch you' rise.

All too soon,
as the bait-maker's story goes,
the last gull gave
a john crow warning,
and the time came:
"*. . . for your greed to ooze out
on the streets,
for your gains to bleed down
on the sand,
for your eyes to look up,
and your split spirit to slip away fast,
under the weight
of your own
blood, doubloons and lace;
to slip away fast,
then cling like lice,
like cranny-dust;
blood, doubloons and lace . . .*"

The misery of your people
hung like masks
on the wooden stakes
along the palisades;
it stretched across the Harbour;
it met the short sighs
from Gallows Point.

The guango buried her pride
and died
beside the spathodias.

Port Royal,
I see you
sweating
in your wealth;
I see your loaded wharves,
waiting,
lopsided
with loot;
Peru left
with a slit throat;
Mexico maimed.

I hear
the belching roar
sliding
from under the distant foothills,
shaking the earth
in caterpillar scallops,
vibrating through Bath
to the beaches;

and Caribbea,
fathoms down,
tearing her elemental calm
in a mounting concussion,

spitting splinters of houses,
and flinging the *Swan*
across her heaped furrows.

I know your pain;
I know about your past;
I know, too,
the finality of your surrender;
I imagine the dislocated bodies,
the float of shoals
of destruction
lying along the port;

your arms,
deeper than ravines,
sank into the sea;

and angry,
yet maternal,
you gave room
to everything,
Caribbea,
and everything
was drowned
inside you,
witness
of our transition;

but
remember,
I know your pain;
I know about your past.

Our Sea,
prepare a path.

You've told us so much;
you've shown us how
the rain-forest is a warehouse
for the Maku
and the river the same
for the Barasana,
wedged in North West Amazonia;
you've shown us how
they both own
very little,
next to nothing but their souls;
and they move fast;
they say that
the faithful *curare*
glints in the eye
of the dropped pig.

Caribbea,
prepare that path.

Port Royal,
flawed peninsula,
very nearly
an offshore island,

I know those bruised knots
in the wood,
the upright post and arm
on which the bodies dangled;
I still see the raked sand.

I know your pain;
I know about your past.

I know I should know that
the lime flowers
will make us sleep,

and that
I should also know
exactly when to pick them.

Palizada
of all sorts,
you began to sink
jus' when you was a-ketch you' rise.

Today,
the bait-maker talks
about your pirate ways,
your gold plates at altar rails,
the rotting fish on splintered roadways,
cathedral bells bellowing deep in sea-bowels,
screech of siren fish scalloping a violent sea.

You
and Caribbea
have told us so much;
you've shown us how
the Maku
and the Barasana own
very little,

next to nothing but their souls;
how they move fast;
and how they say that
the faithful *curare*
glints in the eye
of the dropped pig.

Caribbea,
prepare that path.

Because of 1796

Sing a simple song of bloodshed,
plantocratic economics,
plantation morality,
latifundist tricks
and bird-song: leave these
to an orphan, in the heartland,
an he'll hear crested quail doves,
blue quits and coffee terns
singing their circular critical monotone;
he'll see homing birds
and no sight of home;
he'll hear desperate birdtone;

black birds, white-trumpeted datura
fringing the lanes;
the rain bird forgetting to moan;
the grass snake stitching its way
across the crisp bramble;
the slow push of fresh weeds taking root;
another morning and another faster nightfall,
and another faster morning;

he'll see the spread of suppression,
Maroon heads, cumulus-heaped,
shifting, dipping;
and below,
Caribbea bubbling to froth
and keeping low under the cry
of hoarse throats:

Rebellion!
Rebellion!
Rebellion!

Clawt the spell!
Backra man hell!
Dead go tell!

And there are the barracoon tears
for freedom
and the dream of the blaze
of broken bracelets;

and there are the night owls
blinking at the harvest
of resentment,
while action and freedom,
graceless as ever,
dig gullies to the hills,
as alien blood soaks
the stunted grass;

then,
the slick swoop
of john crows,
cutting flesh from bone,
while black machetes
mince a path
through tangled tracks;

(Caribbea,
tell us:
is there no growth
where the land is denied
destruction?)

after the intemperate policies
of Balcarres (so described at the time
of his crime),
Nova Scotia heard thumping Maroon feet
and Sierra Leone opened once again her arms;

Great Cockpit Country,
moon-faced refuge,
pitted, remote,
where,
on Cima and Cimaron,
Gun Hill and Garrison Point
stand like Lucia's Pitons,
lean watchmen over a field
irreparable distress;

and those beaten
overseas men
with their well-written treaties,
those cunning pieces of paper,
more deadly than quick poison;

to explain the treachery
and the collaboration
of the mountain men,
the old fighter said that
a defeated people
have no loyalties;
some storytellers
and singers
have a rare compassion;

know you're dear to me,
Caribbea;

you know it all;
you know the torment,
the theft;

you know the masked tensions
and the clear days;

for the binding
is in the breaking,

and the broken people
profit from the struggle;

I can only guess
at the last moment
just how special
the stratagem
must have been;

I can only imagine
I hold those years
in my head;
I can only imagine
I hear:

Rebellion!
Rebellion!
Rebellion!

There are so many,
so very many remains
of our great ancestors lying
next to the soles of our feet
as we mine bauxite
or take a tourist's arm
or walk aimlessly
over the sites
of old plantations
that the generations
are easily able to make
the necessary connection,
if they're inclined,
with a smile
or a knowing shrug
but always, always,
with some sort of recognition.

Rebellion!
Rebellion!
Rebellion!

The women of the dead men
would hesitate, at first,
pause,
move slightly forward,
but, again, hesitate
to fuck with the lucky men,
safely,
left behind,
blameless hogs in cocoa patches;
but, soon, they'd yield,
if only to slice away
the loneliness they'd inherited
from their dead men
and
if only to smash
the solitude of the Middle Passage.

Turning and twisting,
salivating, grimacing,
under the blind urgency
of their new men,
sugar wasn't sweet
for the women
whom the generations hardly dream about;
it had entered their blood,
like a lurking tape worm,
and changed their world; and
it is still exploding in ours.

Today,
the hopeful leap

and lift their women's dresses
and part their thighs
and stream their hands
along the soft insides
of a mystery of pain,
humiliation
and terrifying loss.
Whiplash scars meet
the fever of the young men's finger-tips.
And molasses stains. And gravel marks.
And the clinging pollen
on the black earth,
on the red dirt,
where their women had
only recently
been thrown and brutalised.

One woman looks up.
For me, her smile
and later her piercing groan
reduced
the boiler house
and the vast acreage of plantation
to a fistful of sand.

Rebellion!
Rebellion!
Rebellion!

Because of 1833

And there are the dreams,
the waving corn,
free red hairs,
loose in the Undertaker Wind
that haunted Quashie's adobe huts;

there are the sessions
to which Clarkson and Wilberforce
were denied admission: SLAVES ONLY

Other things slip
into these dreams:
a stifled laugh,
a small gesture towards a grand veranda;
and the dreamers shift
on torn skin;
vines, bitter cords,
strap sweet hopes,
while blindfolds drop
near our feet:
the bleary-eyed stumbling
in the half-light,
and latifundia profits
crash down
like quarry stones:

for we know one backyard,
one set o' lash; one life we know;
'cause is that all a-weekday time we did know . . .

nursing bucking urges
like blistered feet;
wanting to run
the length of the land:

'cause is that all a-weekday time we did know . . .

yet,
there are the other tears,
pride, propriety,
and the jangling chains
replaced by different noises:

bitterness,
acute suspects
(hanging around
the boiler house),
acute suspicions,
complexes
(the jangling never
really stopped);
natural right of independent thought,
economics aside,
freedom to choose a burial spot,
freedom to live, freedom to die:

we free! we free!
Lawd, today, we free!

A wash of light,
a swift kitchen knife!
Stupefaction, slice, slice,
disengaging thunderclap,
hammer on anvil (a different symbol,
now), a new position,
a groundin';

a voice asks for a path,
a path for those on their way,
a path with milestones
they'll make
as they go:

we free! we free!
Lawd, today, we free!

Caribbea,
even now,
know we ask;
prepare a path.

Caribbea,
prepare a path.

Consider
the case o' Country,
the lonlies' man
in town.

Country jook the mornin'
wit' him finger,
an' ask the 'cestors them:
you did ever talk to the lan'?
You did ever talk real serious to it?
You been diggin' into it, from Africa,
an' you sleep right 'pon top o' it,
since you come,
an' you been slap nex' to dutty
all you' slavin' life. That no lie!
But, you did ever talk real serious to it?
You ever hear what it say 'bout freedom
an' the ways it got,
open up sometimes, sometimes p'rhaps not,
foot into door, ankle get chop off,
sun hot, cold night?

Freedom is as freedom does,
and it didn't accomplish much.

Take that up to the quarry,
and put it to the test.

"Free is shit,"
the man with the shovel said,
bending over and scooping up
the diced quarry pebbles

which were burying
his dusty scaled ankles,
and making a mechanical man of him.

"Free is when them gone,
an' you' lan' come back home
to you in one piece;
free is when them gone f'true,
when them lif' up an' fly 'way like wasp,
when them shadow *x* itself out,
an' you' lan' wrap it two han' roun' you
wit' love," he said, putting a pebble
between his teeth and promising himself
to start discovering the new alternative
he'd had in his thoughts
from first light that morning.

"Free is when you' yard
only grow f'you own rich mineral,
f'you own sugar cane an' banana,
an' f'you own dandelion tea,
an' when the groun' spread out
an' is f'you own,
in life an' deat',
top an' bottom;
everyt'ing else,
any which way or ever,
is one self-foolin'
kind o' mirror."

He stepped out
of the quarry pebbles,
spat,
clasped his hands
into a bunched fist,
raised it to his lips,
blew a tune over it,
smiled (like his Port Antonio cousin
would certainly have
with his face turned away
from the loaded ship),
and said, "I always countin' somebody else benefits,
stackin' somebody else foreign balance,
livin' in somebody else hopes,
walkin' in somebody else clothes.
Is what them think this is, any at all?
Life don't go so."

He walked
slowly
out to the open road,
beat the quarry dust
out of his shirt,
stamped his boots
hard on the baked marl,
and said, "Fight me an' lose,
an' give me back me lan'
an' give me back me sea
an' give me back me free,
right now."

Caribbea,
prepare that path.

Because of 1865

Caribbea,
you heard the long, drawn-out cries
from Stony Gut,
the muffled shouts
from ackee-mouths,
pursed and pink,
the lament of the young women,
the tight grunting
of the old people
huddled round the stand-pipe;

you saw the dance round the Bay,
round Bogle's name,
across the planters' lawns;

you know the quarrel:
you did listen Baptis' Bell;

you know how Quashie's Grievances
were settled in blood
that washed *the white quill whiter;*

you've stayed with the night-watch
and jabbed the light off the hill
with nervous bayonets;

but Caribbea,
you, too, have counted
the hours in the Bay,
and the many uses
of the love of sunshine
in midday vestibules,
the many uses
of the clammy shrug
in the early evening;

Caribbea,
you turned away
and back again;
you stayed another night;

your anguish made
the mountain-witch sing;
you felt the suck of time;
you sucked the acid rind;
you felt the pain of the past.

That Paul Bogle man:
the way them murder him, eh?

That Paul, Brother Man:
a natural lover o' freedom,
justice an' lan'!

An' Gordon, G. W. Gordon,
hangin' up so,
witness Bath floggin',
shootin', neck-breakin',
burnin' (a t'ousan' 'ouse
an' more): all o' it do
by Eyre army an' navy.
Ask wavy hair Gordon ghos'!

An' that ill-use Edward John Eyre,
born hero, Governor,
born murderer: is where he gone,
right man in the right place?

An' that *rass*, Carlyle,
wit' him Nigger Question
an' him twis'-up, rancid brain!

Caribbea,
you've collected the horror
of the shock waves
in St. Thomas-in-the-East;
you've touched the fissure traces
throughout the land;
you've felt the sympathetic tremors,
the split-second reactions,
the outbursts in solidarity;
you've seen the stone-peppered
out-houses,
the fired cane-rows,
the ripped-off bits
of *broderie Anglaise.*

You know it all:
Missis Queen,
livin' off o' we,
over the water;
her Scotsman overseer,
Newgate recidivis',
whip-han' white stud,
Black 'oman molester,
tormentor, violator;

Carlyle "Discourse on Niggers",
FRASER MAGAZINE
(the centre page floatin'
in a lily pond
back o' Golden Grove
Great House);
tear-up osnaburg
sackin' cloth;
wasted plantations,

buggered economy;
the Scotch attorney son,
Vestryman Gordon,
brand by Eyre
as a Coloured Landowner,
traitor;
Eyre who did give him blessed name
to one Australian lake,
one Australian peninsula
an' a Jamaican genocide;
Custos Rotulorum
Maximilian von Ketelhodt,
jump-up baron,
Eyre foot-kisser;
Deacon Paul Bogle,
brother o' Moses,
Stony Gut baker,
gatherin' in the Chapel brethren
an' trainin' them
wit' shot-gun an' machete,
in Hordern, Torrington,
Whitehall an' Coley,
an' all over Plantain Garden River valley;
an' then the *Wolverine*
an' Bogle body swingin' free
from the yardarm;
you know it all
like the tattoo-marks
along your sailors' arms.

Caribbea,
prepare a path.

You know, too, that
Quashie went to bed,
in the open,
on the banana trash,
dokunu in the heaped grass,

with revolution
on his mind,
with a taste of change,
like sweet bile,
on his tongue,
with the dirt of the hills
clogged
between his toes,
and
he didn't dream, that night,
of the less than quarter of a bread-loaf
the lives of Black people slide on
or
of the miserable Massa make-do
or even
of Cubba
and the pincer grip
of her yes
and her sunhot love
and her paradise on earth
in Trelawny;
instead, Quashie's dream was about
Cubba's place beside him,
in the new partnership,
the groundin',
in the struggle for freedom, land,
water, own grow an' own slice breadfruit
and a life
without make-do
to hand on
to their children
in the District of Look Behind.

Caribbea,
prepare that path.

Because of 1907

Again,
yet again,
the earth shook, retched,
vomited in disgust
and hurled cobble stones
across the Banyan's shadow;

the worm's spool reached the sky;
the children cried;

a city,
planned for profit,
bared its teeth
and sprang
for new blood;

Kingston's resentment rang
throughout Wareika
and drowned its moans
in Old Plantain Garden;

arrogant buildings,
stanchioned in sugar,
sank hopelessly;
whole townships tottered,
criss-cross,
cross-legged,
while interests
and aspirations slipped away
in the slow slide,
deeper in the yawns of shattered ground,
only to be thrown up again later;

land-larks circled the Harbour
and avoided the fire;
they ignored the dead fish flung ashore,
hurled there, as if to mock
the crippled fishermen;
wise birds that they are
they saw the smirk
that the Old Woman forgot
to wipe from her face
before her prophecy
had come to an end
beyond Newcastle's folds.

Kingston,
your commercial sun
turned its brightest coin
back on you;

the reports say
your loss was great;
your material plans splintered;

but,
there was no comforting space
for you
between Caribbea's breasts;

I talk about your desolation;
I feel your shame.

Caribbea,
Our Sea,
prepare that path
on which your new men may walk,
where we may find

a constant guide
along your maternal shore;

direct the fire
to the ground
over which the parasitic bush grows;

lean your breasts, once more,
towards our torn mouths;
press the milk into our faces;
clean our eyes;
set our growth;

hear us,
now that we ask;
now that we hunger,
hear us.

Caribbea,
knowledgeable,
patient,

raise your emancipated arms;
give your breasts,

maternal,
absolute,
elegant,
malachite eyes.

I talk about your desolation;
I feel your shame.

I keep seeing the grab marks,
the scars the thieves leave behind,
the slashes,
the lacerated fidelities,
the trampled women,
the sold men,
the murdered calm,

the madness,
and I nod my pride
at your strength.

I watch the poorest of my people
walking the streets,
and they walk like sucked seeds,
like the flecks
of useless weeds
brushed from the shoulders
of well-made suits.

Our lives are cracked.
The whip misses, once,
and scores the ground instead.

Our backs rejoice!
But down comes the whip again.

If this is all we may expect;
if this is all our lives will get;
if this is our hell, our home;
then,
we'll stamp out the marks,
cover the scars,
stitch the slashes,
wattle an' daub the cracks,
lift up our women,
restore our men,
return the calm
and use the madness
to shore up our strength
and yours.

Caribbea,
direct the fire
to the ground
over which the parasitic bush grows;

lean your breasts, once more,
towards our torn mouths;
press the milk into our faces;
clean our eyes;
set our growth;

hear us,
now that we ask;
now that we hunger,
hear us.

Caribbea,
knowledgeable,
patient,

raise your emancipated arms;
give your breasts,

maternal,
absolute,
elegant,
malachite eyes.

Caribbea,
prepare that path.

3

Mento Time

Saturday in Kingston
The Banyan
Joshua and Emmanuel

The Baton of unlawful law and the deafness of Black souls have dimmed the Churchical sounds. Yet, Ossie's gay, festive beat I full appreciate; it's the child of countless, of mine, for when from some juke-box, gully-side or captured lot moves the pulsing dance of the Ke-Te rhythm, then, also in me stirs the African Lance.

Audvil King From 'The Awakening' in ONE LOVE

Saturday in Kingston

(i)

Instead
of tinkering
with the darkness,
adjusting to dispossession,
I trample it;
I trample death.

I join two possessions;
I join self, one gift,
with hope, the other,
and use the union
like a pile driver.

I trample death
with birthfeet;
I leave the foreshore
for the hills;

Wareika,
my birth after my death!

Cold cash,
attempts at whiteness,
an extended line of class
and neon lighting
will dazzle us
like Tacuma's suggestion to pass
when things are thin in the skin.

Mento beat!
Shey-shey feet!

(ii)

There was the memory
of a murderous journey
locked in the core
of the drums,
slaughter with staring eyes,
brilliant eyes,
Diaspora wide,
blood pulsing
to *mento* strength.

Shey-shey feet!

Cold cash!

I woke up with Kingston
and heard the new day stirring,
strumming
Costa Rica Charlie
big time banjo,
big like any piano,
under them fenky-fenky fingers
he sportin' wit' the gol' ring
an' gol' teet' in him mout';
when Charlie lick the strings,
you fenay grease.

It was a long time ago,
when I walked with the morning wind.

There was no hidden eye
among the limp joseph's-coat.

I walked with my back to the whistling
of the Harbour breezes;
I stepped hard on history
like a cool customer
crunching down
on dry calabash skins,
and then I spun round
and faced Victoria Pier.

I walked down Upper King Street
and listened to a story
about two imported
investment experts,
guests from Canaan,
who'd been heard describing the potential
of ". . . the plump, high bottoms
and long thighs
of these Black bitches."
It was a short, sharp fight,
the storyteller said.
A possessive swipe or two
of an iron bar
and the investment experts
were floating assets.

I picked up scraps of conversations,
customary monologues,
calculated confessions,
light lip-stick laughter,
giggles about last night's party,
happenings in a new American historical novel,
incidents from the latest middle-class adulteries,
more giggles, giggles of incidents
that never occurred, wicked suspicions,
evil overstatements, downright lies,
slanderous personal histories
and a gross of assorted
Kong's Grocery gossip.

I saw arms fondled
like mangoes at Parade,
and heard more giggles
at People's Mart.

Community Store
was low-keyed,
plush with luxury items,
and cooled
by slow-moving electric fans
like large whirring spiders.

There was no hidden eye.
I passed schoolboy, milkman,
sweet girl, housewife, pauper,
Rasta,
and their arms and legs
were as loose-limbed as the Colony;
a downtown girl
rolled her hips,
sprung on marble-ball feet,
and grinned
and began selecting
her Saturday night friend;
there was a gradually increased speed
in her twist of neck
and flick of finger-tip;
there was a trick of rhythm
in her view of the world,
a doubt-excluding bounce
in her step;
the sidewalk
slipped away unnoticed,
under her vaseline smooth
patent-leather shoes,
as sidewalks should
under a downtown girl;

then,
there was her partner, sweet boy,
willowy as a bleached eucalyptus,
redibo to a turn,
sure of his reward
as the ramgoat blossom
its early display:
if plum goin' fall,
make it fall down
right yah-so, sof',
sof' an' willin'.

I followed them
through the clang of traffic,
banging of closing stores,
across Parade,
through the parked buses,
all the way along King Street,
and down to Victoria Pier.

The Harbour water
floated a few tight screws
of wood shavings,
cigarette packets
and soggy wrapping paper cut-outs,
launched recently
by four boys
playing their noisy
boa'd 'orse regatta.

A spike of sunlight
stabbed a plank
at the end of the Pier.

Mento beat!

(iii)

I walked up Temple Lane,
to Snappy's
with its persistence of dried shrimps,
booby eggs,
heated-over patties,
over-heated half-day workers,
stale beer;
Costa Rica Charlie
was on spot,
impressive as life.

I wished away the sourness
of the outside lavatory,
the shrill cacophony
of the peanut vendor.

Icilda Smallpiece
crunched a shell
and cursed the man
for selling plausible empties:
"Is what the *rass* you take me for, eh?
Mus' a touris', nuh?"

A sailor moved closer to the counter
than he had been
for some minutes,
and was warned:
"A.B., that barmaid not for sale, you know.
She can't pour out like Dagger Rum.
So, hold on to you' brush,
'case you lose it in the rush!"

Two student-cadets,
stalking under blinking eyelids,
parched about the lashes
with parade dust,
bought loose cigarettes
and slipped away,
as a beggar, in a military tunic,
dragging his amputation behind him,
approached,
with half an oath,
half a plea:
"See Gawd, dey! I 'ungry, you see.
I 'ungry bad, bad.
Gi'e me a copper, nuh?
That's all; a copper to live."

I looked at the regiment
of rum bottles,
at the vivid labels,
and saw two cane-cutters
carrying bundles
on most of them,
and heard:
"Massa, we workin';
we still workin' 'ard for you!"
I thought of black shoulders
under cutting lashes
instead of black faces
grinning on rum bottles.

A Three Card man asked:
"If you think you bad,
find me Queen-o'-Spades!"

King-pin Boysie Smart
cupped his prick and balls
and shuffled proudly up
to Icilda; she glared at him
like death; it was an obvious present
she could do without.

Mento beat!

Rockin' up, rockin' down,
tackin' straight, skirtin' roun';
rockin' shoulder-rock,
glidin' 'ead-an'-elbow rock;
jumpin' up, circlin' down,
shey-shey roun' the town!

Down Temple Lane,
the drums were beating brass
in the shattered drinkers' heads;
the drums blared like sudden eyes,
eyes that bulged,
brilliant eyes, like suneyes,
dancing, eardrum-thumping eyes,
lunatic, *ganja* eyes,
bongo eyes;
head, hips and hands
smashed Caliban!

Play down to dead earth,
bongo drum;
bring blood to *mento* strength!

Feet,
stabbing spines in the dance,
beat your cane tapestry of thuds;

pound down, grass feet,
soft in sweeter rhythms!

Wrists twist in angel shapes;
jutting, butting foreheads
jerk and spin beads of sweat.

Mento beat!

(iv)

I imagine
I'm there
sitting in a broken chair,
its cane seat as penetrated
as San Juan.

I've just passed a pool of vomit
released from a crater-mouthed rummer,
an anti-materialist, an egalitarian,
a private radical among his own post-Victorian
authoritarian school-teaching peers
in Lower St. Andrew.
But, who would know that about him?
He was drunk nearly all the time.
Catch him sober (during the briefest spasm
of abject depression) and he'd tell you:
"Nothing to join and become part of, really.
No oneness, anywhere. Things are so fragmented.
It's hopeless."

I take in everything
in a deliberate swivel,
in simple good faith,
neither loathing the scene
nor complaining.

I swallow everything
with rum and water:
the swish of luminous taffeta,
rustle and crackle
of cheap nylon frocks,
spirals of smoke
from twitching mouth-corners on the slope,
from painted-over nicotine-tinted lips;
I swallow the stains, the hurts, slights,
regrets, everything.

I watch the self-consciously posed
civil service cigarette-holders,
trembling forefingers
in the dance of point-making,
nervous attempts at informed small talk
torn, desperately, from TIME
and reliable British Council publications.

I count the traceries of condensation
running slowly down chilled beer bottles.

Who can avoid the plaintive notes
from the hungry clarinettist,
half belching, half living,
under the drone
of five-shilling whores,
gnarled brambles
of young women
pitching frothy,
curling tobacco ash
into over-stuffed ashtrays?

Who can miss the freelance traders
marketing burst fruit and promises,
amateurs jockeying
with stalwart professionals
and getting the worst of it?

Who can ignore the smell
of urine passing, squelched,
under dispassionately plastered
Vanishing Cream?

We walk on,
from rum to rum.

We all pretend
not to recognise
the nausea
of the night-out.

We live in a Colony.
Soon, we'll be neo-colonials.

We walk on.

The hard beat
of the newspaper vendors
comes like the phoenix flapping,
slapping the SUNDAY GLEANER
into the chipped concrete
next to drowsing offices;
the folded thud fuses
with the flatness
of the dying mock-*calypso* rhythms
and *mento* tunes;
suddenly, a swarm of sounds
fills the collapsed hearts,
the blighted illusions,
the empty pockets,
and holds out a clip-joint rainbow
scooped out of the splinters
of rum and water and melded echoes:
so, duck you' 'ead an' shake you' spine
an' make her shake her body-line;
hold her han' an' squeeze her tight
an' make her know is she tonight;

get in firs' an' get in 'ard
an' make you' stan' like man-o'-yard!

I trample death
with birthfeet;
I leave the foreshore
for the hills;

Wareika,
my birth after my death!

Cold cash,
attempts at whiteness,
an extended line of class
and neon lighting
will dazzle us
like Tacuma's suggestion to pass
when things are thin in the skin.

Mento beat!
Shey-shey feet!

The Banyan

(i)

The sun razored into Kingston.
The sliced Park sprawled out of breath.
Nuzzling newsprint wrapped the feet
of the low wooden benches.
The buttercups on the north west corner
were sun-blasted cockle shells.

An old man and a boy spat
and the earth curled parched fingers
around the two small puddles,
pop-eyed relics of the heat.

A rapid conveyor-belt
of glinting metal,
white-walled tyres,
ordinary service greys
and warped handcart iron wheels
lashed King Street.

The point-duty policeman
flashed angry gloved hands
which grew and grew.

(ii)

I looked back at the Park
and gazed at the Banyan stump,
an abandoned peg leg,
an ugly hulk all its own
in the dry dirt.

I watched the spot
where the Giant Banyan had stood,
muscular, maternal uncle,
spreading witness
to all the historical charges,
dark green in the comfortless years,

and knew
that the children
would still continue
to play
roun' a knobbiness.

I knew
that other early griefs
had watered its adventitious roots;
that it had witnessed the new morning,
not like the other false alarms
but the start of the new alternative.

I saw the john crows circling
where, once, they knew shelter
in the bulky coils of branches;
but they remained a short time:
the branches them stay a quako time,
one merry, merry, short quako time.

The crows saw the emptiness,
the knobbiness,
and they knew that
there had been a death,
as if the demanding history teacher
had come and gone,
time and again,
as if the Park
had never stood still
at any time;
and they flew on
through cirrus clouds
baffled about the body
that wasn't:
'bout the body that wasn't 'bout
that wasn't 'bout, at all.

(iii)

I walked on
remembering the band concerts on Sundays,
when the boys believed and played
roun' an' roun' a knobbiness.

I walked on
remembering the band concerts,
again and again,
when the Banyan hung
that tricky drapery of vines
and the boys played hide-an'-seek
among its continental roots.

I remembered the time
when we all believed and played
roun' an' roun' a knobbiness.

I remembered the old *cavatinas*,
simple songs
translated slowly
and emotionally
to fit our afternoon needs.

I remembered the over-crowded *scrambolas*,
blunt-nosed and sturdy all over,
parked near by,
ready for the country roads.

I remembered the Sundays
like the taste of stolen *brawta*,
over-ripe naseberries:
the pulp did stay a quako time,
one merry, merry, short quako time.

That Park!
That Park and the boys
(and even the grown men,
so described by their passing critics)
and how we believed and played
'bout the body that wasn't 'bout
that wasn't 'bout, at all!

All through the years,
in those days,
Aunt Pearl's newly-laid eggs
were things for explosions;
drop an artefact
and it would become a plaything;

rules were for the governed,
and that tall bird-man,
plumed, spotless white,
in King's House,
Massa Langgulala,
seemed ages away from the Park,
though it was named
after Missis S'm'body Queen
who might have been
his grand employer
had he descended on us
much earlier than he had;
bad games were all we played,
in those days,
or so we thought.

Track down
Park Lawyer Bonitto,
a staunch Garvey man,
UNIA from way, way back,
and he'll tell you that,
lookin' over the years,
it was a good place to go to,
a sweet, free set-up,
a poor people Park,
where you could talk you' talk
an' ease you' brain
whatever comin' on
shapin' like pain;
where you could lick up you' politics,
take all sort o' strain,
walk 'bout, kick stone,
cuss *rass*, pick bone
wit' anybody you like
an' nobody would know
a Gawd t'ing;

talk you' talk, yes,
an' talk it strong
wit'out a single soul wrong;
yet an' all though,
it was somebody safety valve,
a way f'make conscience salve
an' keep down the dus' from flyin'.

Cool breeze!

I walked on
and remembered:
"I bet I box you!
You wouldn' venture!
A Lawdie Gawdie
Giggy Wappy
belly lick'm skid'm
I buy Jacob
never miss an' pu' down
Mother White fry fish!"

Among,
between,
beside your roots:
Giant Banyan.

I walked on
and remembered:
is how the *rass* man
wit' the whip did say it,
again?
How?

"These fuckin' people,
fucked as they are,
fuckin' well believe
in immortality.
It's my right and duty
to give them back
a sense of death!"

Joshua and Emmanuel

(i)

Old Man Joshua sucked hard
on his clay pipe
and asked his friend,
"Manny, 'member Rodney Memorial Park,
some years back?"

Emmanuel led with the corner
of his right eye, winked,
nodded ages,
spat yellow phlegm
and reassured Joshua,
"Them was the days that
Spanish Town was really Spanish Town, Josh.
True word that!"

Joshua,
Emmanuel
and the Firs' o' Augus' Celebrations
in the Old Capital:
another Banyan conversation
everybody had heard
who knew the two old men,
their ancient narrative,
their sunset clay pipe.

Joshua and Emmanuel
drew closer to each other,
ol'-time experience
touchin' ol'-time experience,
in a cool corner of the Park;
they wheezed,
and shrewd chuckles darted
between them
like thumb-flicked guinep seeds.

(ii)

Joshua: There was the shadow o' suppression liftin'
off the lan', Manny, off the lan'
by coffee-'edge an' Manor outroom.
Roun' the grassyard an' roun' the Market Place,
Abolition Act was the subjec',
bright, bright all 'bout,
like them Sunday suit
after the weeks an' weeks
o' them Sunday rains.

The shadow had lifted
and there were very slow feet
in the Square;
the yolk had snapped,
cracked down its back,
but the feet fumbled
in the dance,
either ignorant of the tune
or dispossessed of the beat.

Emmanuel: You know somet'ing, Josh?
Jerk you' mem'ries far back,
an' try 'pare them days wit' these
we livin' 'mongst, now, today.

Joshua: Diff'rent times
an' diff'rent disposition
overtake we, Manny.

Emmanuel: Look how them bwoy an' gal pickney,
these days, jumpin' wit' joy,
as if joy is common item,
like rockstone a' riverbottom,
easy f'collec'.

Joshua: 'Member how that same time
was a rygin time, Manny?

Emmanuel: 'Member how that Augus'
f'we own cripple-up 'cestors
mus' be did jump wit' joy
when joy was really joy?

Joshua: Manny, I tell you,
times change colour bad.

Emmanuel: Times change bad f'true, Josh.
Them change from a luscious redfruit
into a dutty, dutty brown,
like gutter water.

Joshua: Ol' Spanish Town
actual gone far from we,
though everybody singin' still.
The voice them never stop.
But, go listen
what them singin', Manny!
It sad. It sad bad f'true.

Emmanuel: Sad bad, Josh!

Joshua: Some tune mellow wit' years
like how them say good rum
does do in a cask
goin' two which way
'cross the Atlantic.

Emmanuel: True word, Josh,
but mellow sometimes
is another word for spoil.
'Member, Farmer Bwoy cow 'ave calf in haste
an' calf fat while cow dead,
drop down 'pon bankside, jus' so.

Joshua: True word, Manny.
Mos' true word that.

Emmanuel: Glad you 'gree, Josh.
Glad you 'gree.

Joshua: Mus' an' boun' to 'gree, Manny.
A man like me know how this t'ing go
from mornin', yes.
Mus' an' boun' to 'gree, Manny.

Emmanuel: How 'bout the bwoy an' gal pickney them?
How them stay?

Joshua: Them findin' out, Manny.
Them findin' out f'themself.

There were borrowed,
half-learned,
incomplete hosannas
in the name
San Jago de la Vega;
there were mimetic cries
for the Old Capital,
outpourings without a plan,
without resolution,
without trust,
without faith.

There were feet,
clapping the air
like aimless flails,
feet intended to beat
and batter clay
on a hard, long trek.

Emmanuel: You talk 'bout problems!
We got plenty o' those, Josh.
We got all sorts.
Take the language t'ing, now,
as f'instance!
It not even f'we own
proper yet.

Look how we force
f'fingle wit' it
when we want
f'write as we talk;
look how much mark an' stop
we got f'drop
'pon top o' it
when we write it down!

Joshua: Is only one reason cause that.
F'we tongue still tie up
wit' that other somet'ing
which we still oblige f'use
as a secon' base after Africa
an' the other Motherlan' them.

Emmanuel: All the same, though,
we got few word well
that is f'we own
from firs' base.

Joshua: But, mos' make out o' f'them
Englishman talkin'
when them lan' we up
right yah so 'pon the rock.

Emmanuel: Short lesson
f'the bwoy an' gal them
is this:
we got to rip 'way clean,
one day name day,
if it get *all* the people them
doin' the rippin' same time
as the new buildin' goin' up.

Joshua: But, Manny,
is a big rip an' buil' that?

Emmanuel: So what you think
rip an' buil' is for
if you decide f'do it?
Rip an' buil' got to big
if is business you mean.

Bruck up the far back spell,
bullyrige the belly cord,
bragadap the control
an' cause some healthy bangarangs!
Dance Combolo wit' you' combolo pasero,
find the power,
set up a new set-up
an' take charge!

Joshua: Manny, the worl' not easy.
Mos' t'ings end up into power.
How we an' power stay?

Emmanuel: As how I see t'ings,
power is the lan'
an' the lan' is natural.
Now, then,
look all roun' we!
Don't you see
that we got the natural
right roun' we?
So, the t'ing is f'get
the natural back to we,
back in f'we han',
sticky 'pon f'we finger them!

Joshua: How I see it, Manny,
is like this:
power is seepage,
pure an' simple seepage,
slow or quick,
which ever way
you can capture it.

Now, that is the politics
you got f'study you' brains
f'find out an' use.
The lan' is a natural t'ing.
But power is what
we make wit' moves
an' what we move wit'
'cross the lan',
same so, day into day.

Emmanuel: You think the bwoy them
in the big chair
back o' the broad desk
got seepage
which ever way?

Joshua: I would say
them learnin'.

Emmanuel: An' I would say
the others learnin', too,
if I know this history trap
we livin' into.

Joshua: We all learnin'.

Emmanuel: Some more than others.

Joshua: The natural bwoy them
got to be the some.

Emmanuel: Or else what?

Joshua: Or else the corn meal pone
goin' get finish,
nyam off, one time,
an' everybody belly goin' empty,
an' everybody goin' get capture,
an' we won't 'ave
not even weself lef' on the lan'.

The two old men nodded to each other
and their voices continued
licking the time of year;
their words were runaway horses.

(iii)

I trample death
with birthfeet;
I leave the foreshore
for the hills;

Wareika,
my birth after my death!

Cold cash,
attempts at whiteness,
an extended line of class
and neon lighting
will dazzle us
like Tacuma's suggestion to pass
when things are thin in the skin.

Mento beat!
Shey-shey feet!

4

Caribbean Petchary

Upheaval 1938
New Constitution 1944
Hurricane 1951
Caribbean Petchary

From the seashore
    to the blue mountain,
    to the roaring ravine,
    we heave our boat.

And the flare in the sky
    opened the night,
    opened the night. . . .

John La Rose From 'Song to an Imperishable Sunlight' in FOUNDATIONS

Who will till this soil
cutting straight fervours into the rock
whose marrow, whose toil

butting into this sweat-sweetened rot
will soften these roots,
loosen the shoots under pebble and shale?

Edward Brathwaite From 'New World, 1; Littoral, IV, 4' in ISLANDS

Upheaval 1938

(i)

A bitch piece o' bangarangs
is jus' what we been waitin' for
since before samba salt fish
use to shingle 'ouse-top;
come '38
an' t'ings goin' bus' like boil,
like so-so pus.

(ii)

Cargo clapper and claw,
Quashie,
finding tomorrow's road,
shouts torment,
swings sticks, flings stones,
Kingston symbols honed
on Sam Browne leather;

years
and years before,
he may not have seen the traps
or recognised the treachery
or fought back fast enough,
but now he slams his shoulders
against the sea
at the brink of the pier
and makes his demands
minus the old acceptable
Churchical sounds;
quilted blackpepper-grain heads
scramble in a wharf hustle
about Busta's windmill fists:

We-will fol-low Bus-ta-man-te!
We-will fol-low Bus-ta-man-te!
We-will fol-low Bus-ta-man-te!
We-will fol-low Bus-ta-man-te,
'til-we-die!

Today,
with yesterday,
at Morant Bay,
tentative feet,
on surer ground
than Stony Gut
and heartpound,
dug
and are digging tracks
of sounding-boards,
throwing free
vibrating signals
like piercing gimlets,
petchary shrieks;
yet,
the voices know nothing
about appeals;
the backs were bent, then,
and are bending, now,
with driving confidence,
bargaining with history,
blow for blow;

and so,
not like grass snakes, lackadaisical,
or turn of street or lane, lackadaisical
like the lackadaisical snail,
but live like trowel-twist
and slash of pathfinder,
the men downtown found eager ground
for their own taking.

(iii)

The Upheaval hacked a clear course,
kicked off a process,
connecting the present year, '38,
with the sixth ahead, '44,
when time-sucked history
fixed its citrus pegs
to Kwasida's mouth
and the juice of the people's labour,
the fretful minutes,
tasted new and sharp
like Seville fruit;

running feet,
like running hopes,
as insistent as *kofi-roba*
going round and round,
resound in an iron pot,
totalling the "vote"
for or against;

it was impossible,
at that time,
to count the accusing fists
and the fires;
but the flames promised to crack
and shatter the colonial looking-glass,
and spike the approaching,
indifferent independence,
the late emancipation,
something like broken glory,
a dragging freedom,
a received liberation:
somebody else's ironic gift;

for there's a freedom
bought with blood and time,
blood and time anywhere mixed,
time, any time,
blood and time with heads, bloodbent,
picking at tradition like banked leaves,
aware of the dangling cutlass,
like Kikuyu's kicking feet,
Kikuyu screams, Kenyatta's calls.

Our Sea,
prepare that path.

Caribbea,
hear us now.

New Constitution 1944

(i)

Le' we speculate!

An' listen: I know
how late date all this
stocious supposition
goin' look,
but don't make it
bother you.
Jus' elastic-up you' mind
an' stretch touch you' future.

If we like law, our way
(as we say we like it),
an' them gi'e we law, from foreign,
we mus' brace weself f'change it,
jump 'pon top o' it
like springboard
an' dive slap into deep waters.

(ii)

Defiant hibiscus,
everyday shoeblack,
red and white rose mallow,
earthed as shallow as a saucer,
stand firm
beside the torn morning-glory!

Let's all find mahogany
for luck,
and let's shed our slave skin,
a sticking palimpsest,
like ruck!

Grab the new day,
walk straight into the cornbreeze,
beat a conference of pride,
scrap old advice
and plan for change!

Sight of land
after a blind seatrek!
Land sighted!

(iii)

Listen to the mixed murmurs
and recognise the traces
of ashes;

listen to the flapping;
listen to the jack-knifing
of wings,
more wings;
listen to the petchary moving
in the mango tree
next door;
listen!

Caribbea,
lend us your practised ways of surviving,
your profound understanding,
your open house;
Caribbea,
let's hear your warning,
breaking,
washing the time-reefs
between us
and Haiti and Cuba;
let's plumb your solitude,
your depths of stillness,
your philosophic swish of fish;

Caribbea,
prepare a path.

Caribbea,
our strength to fire rachitic limbs,
knowledge for our unsuspecting eyes,
twister of tides,
iron fist for iron times,
sit in with us;
lend us your wisdom;
mother the land
with your understanding;

ever maternal,
absolute,
creative,
prophetic, you,
prepare us
for the hurricane
on the way,
for the fixed stare
of its Eye,
for the free fall,
the long drop!

Caribbea,
knowledgeable,
patient,

raise your emancipated arms;
give your breasts,

maternal,
absolute,
elegant,
malachite eyes.

Our Sea,
prepare a path.

Hurricane 1951

(i)

I remember the night,
black with slack rain,
flaccid when it first began
but with brick drops beating later on
like jump-Poco drumthumps,
beating back the coming morning,
beating with purpose,
routine, rhythm and ritual,
beating like the bounce of batter hide,
hide battered on a shoemaker's block,
batter hide, hide battered,
pane shatter, shattered pane,
batter hide, pane shatter through to dawn.

One bad, sneakin' breeze-blow
take time an' creep up
'pon Joe-Joe life
an' tear him shirt-tail
like bud-feather,
bruck him one-room in two
like chew-stick,
kill him common law wife,
kill him fait'ful goat,
kill him layin'-hen them,
an' go 'way sof', sof' like tief,
like it wasn't causin' no bodders
inside the lan', at all, at all.

(ii)

I remember bridges breaking
like bamboo joints,
between the howl and sizzle of leader wind,
between the sough and sigh of coconut palm.

I remember a small clump
of old women
saying late prayers,
premature thanks,
like busy bees at logwood blossoms.

I remember the lash
and the sting.

Split in Wareika's side!
Slit in Palisadoes!
Crash of commercial Kingston!

The sounds wrenched the city
and howled demon dissonances.

I remember roofless churches
yawning silent litanies;
loose bricks and mortar
were broken teeth;
everywhere the splattered word.

I remember the Old Hope Road Wayside Chapel,
the East Queen Street House of God,
the Mark Lane Temple of the Faithful,
ransacked by the wind,
abject like scattered Christians,
sprawling in the cruel aftermath,
as if expecting some sort of reckoning,
some sort of reckoning.

(iii)

I remember Port Royal, prostrate,
in the traditional position,
poor child
of every pirate's abuse,
spread woman
of a thousand lost sailors'-loves,
rushed to exhaustion,
as if expecting another burial,
another burial.

I remember streets
changed into back yards with matchwood patterns,
back gardens bare like quicklime streets,
bleak, gaping closets,
cluttered gutters,
gutted garrisons.

I remember the agony
gripping the face of the woman
as she stooped over the bloated body
of her dead son, in Trench Town,
the dismembered day,
the sun burning jeers
at naked boys,
and the groans of the survivors
and the shifting shadows
and the irony of property.

I remember the quiet smiles
of the drifting men, women
and small children
as they calculated
the mounds of saturated waste
and inched their way over them
like calliper flies.

I can see the shuffling,
drop-shouldered longshoreman, now,
tattered like a conch shell,
all fringes and nothing else,
bending deep inside a pile of garbage,
his large body, puffed, soft and supple,
withdrawing what to use,
withdrawing what to discard,
withdrawing with confidence,
scraps to start his existence rolling, again,
rolling like the road along the coast.

Caribbea,
knowledgeable,
patient,
light up our bramble path
with your malachite eyes;
bring blood to *mento* strength;

Caribbea,
know we value your love;
know we wait for our survival in you.

Caribbea,
know we ask.

Our Sea,
prepare a path.

Caribbean Petchary

(i)

Petchary!
Petchary!
Petchary!

Yes,
it keeps
stretching
that ceaselessly stabbing
three-syllabled shriek,
belligerent,
pursuing,
black head,
long beak,
fighter,
seventy feet in the air,
heard as *Pitirre* in Cuba
and Puerto Rico,
picked up as *Chicheri*
in the Virgin Islands!

Petchary!
Petchary!
Petchary!

Yes,
again, yes,
responding bird,
enemy of passivity,
scavenger attacker,
machine-gunner,
replier to tyranny!

Petchary is a t'ing
'ard to understan',
'cause it fight up
before it cautious take care;
it raise itself
out o' not'ing,
dive bomb john crow
an' fly straight up
like it mad,
like it makin' magic
look foolish bad!

(ii)

Through tiara blaze,
jewelled plunder dust,
marauding mire of Morgan-lust;

through Port Royal's pestilential years,
through to history's deluge-ducking;

through those and these torrential times,
marked by gold plates at altar rails,
rotting fish on splintered roadways,
cathedral bells bellowing deep in sea-bowels,
screech of siren fish scalloping a violent sea;

through Anancy administrations
of advancing governorships,
expansionist tyrannies,
through scapegoat fancies,
through flash
and fire of revolt,
through Quashie's Grievances,
          Baptist's Pleadings,
          Bogle's squashing Backra's Rulings;

through those
and successive elemental and human thunderclaps,
colonial walls razed to history dust;

through clamour, catchwords,
concocted saviours lasting appointed seasons,
then, slipping into *bourgeois* papa podagric fatigue,
self-regarding hill top affluence;

through wishful thinking,
suddenly arriving oligarchic apathy,
Duke Street prostrations,
visits of disguised aid innovators
tying the already ramified strings
invisibly tighter than their predecessors;

through acts considered favourable
but later proved recklessly wasteful;

through all those
and more,
much, much more,
there was a stirring,
a rustling,
a fluttering aimed
at a concealed horizon:

Petchary!
Petchary!
Petchary!

The land knows those movements well,
the hidden restiveness;
it knows the wake of ashes,
the weight of grave clothes;
it knows the ways of re-birth,
the stillness of death,
the garden magician's wand
of resuscitation;
it has seen its image
in bandages about our bodies;

the land has watched it all,
and so has Caribbea.

Caribbean Petchary,
li'l but talawa!

Caribbean Petchary,
know we move in you;
know we have our being
because of you;
know, too, we expect
your constant stirring,
your constant re-birth!

Caribbean Petchary,
bird of pelican-plenitude,
bird of aggressive attack,
retaliation,
resuscitation,
renewal,
you and Caribbea are one in us;
you are Caribbea!

(iii)

Again,
when through the jagged cracks
in the streets,
Kingston begged
to be spared;

when poinciana clouds piled
and rained egoism
and fragmentation;

when sea-cleft
and tidal rush rose up
and clawed the rubble-city;

when seismic volts
forked the skin
of the Island;

when childcry
and mothercall
were crushed;

Petchary,
you were there;
you were there
when the land-grabbers
planted self-interest
as the foundation stone
of their thin morality;

and Petchary,
you were there,
waiting to rise, again,
waiting to mock death
and destruction, again,
waiting to die
and rise, again!

Count 'pon finger
all the bud we know:
don't is true say
Doctor Bud 'ard bud f'dead?

(iv)

You shot through the turbulence,
the slipped mountain slope,
the severed civic policies,
the tides of high foreign profits
and low local returns;

and we know your brisk flight,
your petcharyessence,
your petcharycalm,
your Caribbean soul,
your universality.

Caribbea,
Caribbean Petchary,
both maternal,
absolute,
define our destiny,
declare our needs,
attend our doubts,
take despair from our doors,
give us back our land,
help us realise our agricultural excellence,
restore our faith!

Those insistent public men?

They really aren't all that important;
they go away, again and again.

Caribbea,
knowledgeable,
patient,

raise your emancipated arms;
give your breasts,

maternal,
absolute,
elegant,
malachite eyes.

Remember,
I know your pain;
I know about your past.

Caribbea,
moving in the morning,
shift your pearls;
bolster the waiting land!

Our Sea,
prepare a path.

Is the lan' I want

(i)

Ol' Cho-Cho Thomas,
a man who understood
the uses of his local library
and ol'-time story power,
would talk to me
about Brazil
and the bad, bad history
of the land, there,
as though he'd been
a Brazilian, first,
and a Kingstonian convert,
long afterwards:
"Time was when Ganga Zumba
liberate up himself
from the wicked plantation o' cane
own by him Portugee slave massa,
walk foot all the way to Palmares
which part him set up
the free tribe o' Zambi,
twenty t'ousan' strong on the lan',
back o' the fores' o' Pernambuco
an' en' up as the one hope
o' all him brethren them
lef' out in bondage.

"The Confederacy o' Palmares,
a real bran' new t'ing for Black people
in those days (an' even for nowadays,
come to think o' it),
stan' 'teady an' talawa
back o' Pernambuco
f'sixty-two years."

(ii)

Cho-Cho was a man
who love *mento*,
back slang,
poetry you talk,
Bible twang,
short-short short story,
news wit' spice an' tone;
Cho-Cho love the lan'
him couldn't own.

Him say
you mus' all listen
inside you 'art-string
to what them singin'
in the yard.
One man:
"I bet I box you!"

'Nother man:
"You wouldn' venture!"

Everybody, same time:
"A Lawdie Gawdie
Giggy Wappy
belly lick'm skid'm
I buy Jacob
never miss an' pu' down
Mother White fry fish!"

(iii)

When John Connu come,
him come wit' style,
wit' pride,
an' wit' plenty noise
an' wit' plenty practice
from way back 'cross plantation lawn

an' 'ill-an'-gully rider.

John Connu got 'orse-'ead an' 'ouse-top
an' king-'ead an' bud-body
an' 'nough other t'ings that frighten
mos' o' we, bad.

John Connu sing
an' John Connu dance
an' Connu walk 'ard
an' Connu walk sof'
an' Connu eye got eyewater into it
when he laugh.

(iv)

Where the one-time Panama Man?
Where he gone?

White suit,
brown-an'-white shoes,
watch chain,
plenty gol' teet',
plenty self,
always feelin' him balls,
Panama Man.

Walkin' 'igh up,
plenty cash,
plenty big talk,
spliff an' so,
spondulicks,
Panama Man.

Li'l Spanish lingo,
li'l Yankee speaky-spokey,
Panama Man.

Watch him movin',
circlin' the town,
lickin' up the dus',
jinglin' him money bag,
tip-an'-pawn Mister Minister Man,
Kingston come back Panama Man.

(v)

An' is what the people pickney singin'?
Is what you think them sayin'?

Them sayin':
"I know somet'ing
I wouldn' tell a man:
corn meal dumplin'
no kill no Negah man!"

An' is what them use to sing?

"Ugly as sin
cawn come in.
Ugly as sin
never go win.
Ugly as sin
Satan son
shoot you'self
wit' a soljah gun!"

An' is what the ol' man sayin'?

"Song-man, dance-man,
ban'-man, clown,
go chance you' chance
roun' the town!"

An' is what the young bwoy sayin'?

"Anancy, spider,
Spider Man,
Wes' African
an' Wes' Indian,
nearish total Caribbean Man!

"You spring out o' you' own 'ead,
'cross Atlantic, over Sargasso,
an' you lan' up 'mongst the pickney them.
You too sweet, Anancy!

"You a travellin' Gawd, yes,
a righteous New Worl' gawd-sen'!

"An' even though them say
you tief bad,
an' you cunnin',
an' you pu' down trap,
an' you get the bes' deal goin',
an' even though you knock sof'ly
an' blow nice when you bite,
you belong, Anancy, Spider Man,
you belong."

An' is what the Locksman sayin'?

"*John Crow keepin' him distance*
an' skinnin' him eye tight, tight.

"Dress up in black,
Peel-neck John Crow
does fly 'igh:
so Bajan people sayin',
all the time.

"But while that turkey
in B'bados takin' time
an' ceilin' 'nough zero,
Jam'can John Crow circlin' deat',
sof' an' low,
an' divin' an' bombin'
the flesh off the freeness
down a' gully bottom
'mongst the san' an' gravel.

"*John Crow spyin' from 'igh
an' shootin' straight 'pon spot.*"

An' is how the phrase catchin' you?

"When puss gone,
empty salt fish barrel makin' so-so noise
an' then ratta take 'ouse
an' cap don't fit
'cause puppy lick you mout'
when you don't take it up.

"Play wit' puppy,
puppy, bad luck like peas,
an' him lose him claw
especial when crab walkin' too much
an' him don't ask fowl pardon.

"So, when cockroach give party,
Backra tief whole estate
'cause Jam'can man only tief
penny-wort' o' lan'."

But the young brothers an' sisters
them say that that shit mus' finish wit' an' done!
Don't is so them say?

"Jack did get him two finger chop off,
simple causin' him get too good
back a' robbin' people t'ings,
lef', right an' centre;
everywhere you look,
you don't see him a *rass!*

"But Jack got so much conceal science
that him ups an' start livin' into a cave,
far from the finger-choppin',
Islan'-grabbin' people,
far up in some 'ill-side place,
far out o' reach.

"An' like how him dead an' gone,
Jack cave holdin' treasure
f'every manjack who sayin' him got 'magination
an' got two, t'ree pickaxe
an' got time f'dig
an' make the 'ill-top drop 'way
an' give up the raw riches to all o' we."

(vi)

An' what 'appen to Bag-an'-Pan
who wouldn' take Jack advice?

"That Bag-an'-Pan!
Him was a Kingston beggar-man,
a proud, bad-temper beggar-man.

"Him drag a tatter-up crocus bag,
a string o' dent-up condense can
an' a clutch o' empty pot;
him walk an' clang;
him frighten everybody
wit' him ghos' bang.

"Him haunt those who taunt him
a' the slightes' chop an' fancy;
an' everybody scamper,
even Anancy,
f'let Bag-an'-Pan drif' cruel,
like a ragged one-man ban',
all over the lan'."

An' Bu'n Down Cross Roads?

"Is so Kingston people still callin' him, yes,
to this very day name day: Bu'n Down Cross Roads,
a walkin' disaster.

"'Cause him really cause
Cross Roads f'bu'n down flat
like cane-piece
dry as chip
when a bad breeze-flulups
blow a' insurance under it.

"Bu'n Down drop a matches-stick
twix' the paper them
an' run.

"Is really Bu'n Down
make Cross Roads bu'n down?"

(vii)

But,
young brothers an' sisters,
is so life actual go?

Is so life go, yes!

"Year start, year en',
the lan' look up an' wait.

"Year start, year en',
the lan' get batter by the slantin' rain,
that soften the brain, the eart',
rot the sugar cane,
wash 'way the top soil,
breed mad mosquito.

"Then, the lan' get flatten by 'urricane,
like pneumatic drill,
that root-up ancient tree an' so,
mash up the 'ouse them,
splinter the sleepers
on the railway track,
drown the population
before you can 'quint.

"An' then, the lan' get crack open wide
by sneakin', scatter-shot drought,
that set fire to 'ill-side farm
an' savanna, in an' out,
bu'n a seam through the sun in the sky
an' whiten the corner o' 'ungry mout'.

"An' yet,
an' still an' all,
the lan' look up!"

Cho-Cho Thomas know all that
by frontin' life wit' a clench fis'
an' a cut aloes bit in him teet'.

(viii)

So, all o' you jus' better start f'make
all the t'ings you use,
'cause the music sayin', "Know you'self!"

The message clear
as MoBay water: "Look inside

an' haul out you'self
an' make a way in the worl',
'cross all the shadows them.
Is only you one you got.
You don't want no help.
You got it
plait up
an' hidin' deep inside you' 'ead.'

Is malachite in the sea!

Yes, Papa D.,
is me this;
is me;
is me an' the sea!

(ix)

Caribbea,
knowledgeable,
patient,

raise your emancipated arms;
give your breasts,

maternal,
absolute,
elegant,
malachite eyes.

Our Sea,
prepare a path.

Caribbea,
know we ask.

Our Sea,
prepare that path.

(x)

All o' we losin' out,
'cause we won't own up to weself,
grab we soul,
grab weself like we know weself,
an' tradition-up we tradition,
an' fuck the nex' man
who laugh after we
an' say it small
an' slave-make
an' fragment-up
an' dark night as Dung'll
an' client-tie
an' don't got no industry
an' no technology.

Fuck him, yes!

Culture come when you buck up
on you'self.
It start when you' body make shadow
on the lan',
an' you know say
that you standin' up into mirror
underneat' you.

I say to meself,
"Is how the *mento* music go?"

You say,
"Is how the river flow?"
or, "How the sea does lay down so?"

I done wit' you.
I into history, now.
Is the lan' I want
an' is the lan'
I out to get.

[Kingston, 1951—London, 1972]